W9-APH-662

Etiquette for Success
Workplace

TITLES IN THE SERIES

Etiquette for Success
Workplace

Sarah Smith

MASON CREST

Mason Crest
450 Parkway Drive, Suite D
Broomall, Pennsylvania PA 19008
(866) MCP-BOOK (toll free)

First printing
9 8 7 6 5 4 3 2 1

ISBN: 978-1-4222-3976-6
Series ISBN: 978-1-4222-3969-8
ebook ISBN: 978-1-4222-7815-4

Cataloging-in-Publication Data on file with the Library of Congress.

Printed and bound in the United States of America.

QR CODES AND LINKS TO THIRD-PARTY CONTENT

Contents

KEY ICONS TO LOOK FOR:

 Words to Understand: These words with their easy-to-understand definitions will increase the reader's understanding of the text while building vocabulary skills.

 Sidebars: This boxed material within the main text allows readers to build knowledge, gain insights, explore possibilities, and broaden their perspectives by weaving together additional information to provide realistic and holistic perspectives.

 Educational Videos: Readers can view videos by scanning our QR codes, providing them with additional content to supplement the text. Examples include news coverage, moments in history, speeches, iconic sports moments, and much more!

 Text-Dependent Questions: These questions send the reader back to the text for more careful attention to the evidence presented there.

 Research Projects: Readers are pointed toward areas of further inquiry connected to each chapter. Suggestions are provided for projects that encourage deeper research and analysis.

 Series Glossary of Key Terms: This back-of-the-book glossary contains terminology used throughout the series. Words found here increase the reader's ability to read and comprehend higher-level books and articles in this field.

Introduction

Dear Reader,

As you read on, you will learn that in any given situation you must be knowledgeable about the expectations set by society regarding your actions and how they will or will not meet the social norms for good manners and etiquette.

It being essential to your success, you learn how your behavior will always be central to how others see you. Unfortunately, many people are judged, or written off almost instantly because of their lack of etiquette.

Times have certainly changed, and while society adapts, you must set your own goals for politeness, good manners, and kindness. All around you there are modern dilemmas to face, but let your good manners set you apart. Start by showing sensitivity toward others, maintain a keen awareness about how those around you feel, and note how your behavior impacts your peers.

Consider that even with changes in the world around you, etiquette must be inclusive and understanding across ages and cultures, and sensitive to your setting. It is important that you take the time to learn; read, practice, and ask questions of those whom you respect. Learn about writing a business letter, sending holiday invitations, or communicating with peers—certain etiquettes should be followed. Is it rude to keep checking your phone during lunch with a friend? Are handwritten thank-you notes still necessary?

It is said that good manners open doors that even the best education cannot. Read on and learn what it takes to make a great first impression.

"No duty is more urgent than that of returning thanks."

"No matter who you are or what you do, your manners will have a direct impact on your professional and social success."

"Respect for ourselves guides our morals; respect for others guides our manners."

"Life is short, but there is always time enough for courtesy."

Words to Understand

career: an occupation undertaken for a significant period of a person's life, with opportunities to progress professionally

etiquette: the customary code of polite behavior among members of a particular profession or group

occupation: a job; a paid position of regular employment

At some point in our lives, most of us will enter the world of employment, whether it be working part-time or full-time. The good manners and etiquette learned at school will then become vital in the workplace. It is a time to show your maturity and to leave any childish behavior behind.

Chapter One
The Importance of Good Etiquette
in the Workplace

As a teenager, you may not be thinking much about getting a job right now. Perhaps school, sports, extracurricular activities, and hanging out with your friends and family take up most of your attention, energy, and time. This is perfectly normal. Not having to worry about paying bills, saving for retirement, and other stressful aspects of adulthood is a great part about being a kid. Enjoy it!

But at some point down the line, you'll be joining the workforce. Whether you take on a part-time job after school, work during college to help pay for your education, or wait until after your schooling is over to begin a new **career**, eventually you'll need (and likely want) to seek out gainful employment.

Why Does Good Etiquette Matter at Work?

Whenever you end up getting a job, hopefully it'll be an **occupation** that you enjoy. Loving what you do (instead of just doing something to make money) can have a huge positive impact on your life and health.

After all, jobs don't just give us an income. They can also give us a sense of purpose and direction. Jobs give us the ability to help others by providing meaningful services and products.

Having a job is also a great way to contribute to your family, community, and society. Plus, a fulfilling job can be a powerful way to express yourself creatively and intellectually.

It is truly a gift to earn a living.

In addition to finding a job you love and one that can help you support the lifestyle you want, it's also wise to understand what it means to have good **etiquette** on the job. Having good etiquette is about

Self-Employment Is an Option—but It's Not for Everyone

Being your own boss sounds nice, but it does come with many unique challenges and stresses. Research from the US Bureau of Labor Statistics actually shows that *fewer* people are self-employed now compared to 10+ years ago. For example, in 2015 the self-employment rate in the US was about 10 percent, whereas in 1994 it was 12 percent.

presenting yourself in a respectable way while also treating others with respect. It is also essential for a long and fruitful career, no matter what profession you choose.

What is Good Etiquette & Why Does It Matter on the Job?

A person with good etiquette has many positive traits and tends to make a good impression on the people around them. These traits include being honest, fair, hardworking, considerate, and good-natured.

In the workplace, people with good etiquette are also seen as professional, cooperative, and dependable. Coworkers, bosses, and customers enjoy being around people who embody these qualities.

Having good etiquette helps you establish a positive work environment among your bosses and colleagues. This makes work more enjoyable, and it can help you be more productive and focused during business hours.

Good etiquette also helps you gain the respect of the people you work with, including customers or clients. This is good for business *and* good for you. For one thing, customers are more loyal to companies (and the people who work for them) who treat them fairly and respectfully. Plus, showing your worth as an employee can increase your chances of career advancement, since your bosses and supervisors may be more likely to select you for a promotion or bonus if you prove yourself to be respectful and hardworking.

Ultimately, having good etiquette in the workplace can make you more appreciated and valued as an employee, and for you this can translate into increased job satisfaction, more opportunities for success, and even greater financial gain.

From the CEO to Custodial Staff, Good Etiquette Counts

Many people start out at entry-level positions when they begin a new job or set out on a new career path. But just because you're new to the workforce doesn't mean that expectations of you are low. If anything, you may have to actually work harder than your

Group discussions are commonplace in today's working environments. Those with good etiquette will be good listeners, allow others to speak, and make any criticism in a polite and constructive way.

colleagues to prove that you are a reliable, trustworthy, productive, and team-oriented employee compared to people who have been on the job for decades.

Perhaps someday you will be in a position where you serve as a supervisor or boss. In fact, many millennials and people from Generation Z/iGeneration (those born 1980–94 and those born in 1995 or later, respectively) are finding ways to be their own boss. They may start a new company or find ways to make money online. Yet even if you are a one-person business, having good etiquette is still important, because you have customers, retailers, and suppliers who depend on you for quality service—and quality treatment.

So no matter what position you fill at your job, it's important to present yourself in a positive way at all times. Whether you are an employee or an employer, having good traits like honesty, fairness, and integrity are critical for your long-term success.

The Importance of Good Etiquette in the Workplace

What to Expect From This Book

You probably act a certain way, dress a certain way, and talk a certain way when you're with your friends and family. While these habits aren't bad, they're generally not appropriate for the workplace. This book will teach you the proper ways to act at work.

Successful businesses are usually run by people with good etiquette skills, who know how to present themselves positively to potential clients. This florist is suitably dressed for the job in hand and is greeting her customer with a friendly smile.

You'll learn the basics first, including how to present yourself well by means of cleanliness, proper dressing, and proper manners.

This book will also cover effective ways to organize your time while at work. Businesses care about productivity, so timekeeping, efficiency, and using a personal diary are all helpful habits. You'll be taught how to communicate and interact with colleagues, clients, customers, and suppliers in a more effective and respectful way. This helps you understand others better and helps you be understood by others, too.

Things in life—and especially at work—aren't always smooth sailing. Knowing what to do in difficult situations is key for good etiquette on the job, so you will be given some ideas on how to resolve problems in the workplace.

For the instances when you may be interacting with your work colleagues in a more casual setting, professional behavior and good etiquette still apply. You'll understand the importance of things like self-control, emotions, and behaviors during social occasions, both in and out of the office.

Finally, you'll learn about appropriate use of office equipment, including work phones, email, computers, fax machines, and more.

Now, whether you're currently employed or still looking for that perfect job, let's "punch in" and begin!

Text-Dependent Questions

1. Why is it beneficial to have a career doing something that you love?

2. Why is important to make a good impression on the people around you in the workplace?

3. Why is important to work hard in an entry-level job?

Research Project

Write a one-page essay on what your perfect career would be. Explain why you would choose that career and why it would make you feel fulfilled.

Words to Understand

attire: clothing, especially of high quality or a formal nature

decision fatigue: deteriorating quality of decisions made by an individual after a long session of decision-making

personal branding: the ongoing process of establishing a certain impression on others about an individual

While you should not feel obligated to spend a lot of money on work attire, it is still crucial to be correctly dressed at work. In some cases, the process of dressing for work is made easier if a uniform is supplied.

Chapter Two
Personal Presentation:
Dressing, Cleanliness &
Good Manners

It doesn't matter if you've had a job for five days or ten years. You should always bring to work at least these two things: respectable **attire** and impeccable manners.

Why? Because maintaining a good appearance and persona is the quickest and easiest way to make a positive first impression on someone, whether that person is your boss, colleague, or a paying customer.

Your Clothes Are Like a Walking Advertisement— for Yourself

Physical appearance has a huge impact in the workplace and is an ongoing process in your **personal branding**. Your clothing, hair, accessories, cleanliness, and your overall style say a lot to other people. Who are you? What is your role in your company? How seriously do you take your job? These and other questions can at least partially be answered by the way you dress and carry yourself on the job.

You should always wear clothing that adheres to your place of employment's specific dress code. You'll probably be given information about the dress code when you are first hired. If you're not sure about whether a certain item of clothing is acceptable, it's better to ask than to guess. Your company's human resources (HR) director or your direct supervisor can usually steer you in the right direction.

Of course, you shouldn't feel obligated to spend a lot of money on work apparel, nor hours and hours getting

When dressing for the office, choose an outfit that is plain, smart, and simple. This office worker is appropriately dressed in a navy suit with a white shirt. Her hair is neatly styled.

Professionalism in the Workplace

ready in the morning. However, if you're starting a new job, be prepared to invest a modest amount of time, money, and energy in your appearance. Looking decent and professional will help you establish a good reputation for yourself.

Uniforms are a Business Expense
Tip: When you are old enough to pay tax, be sure to save your receipts for any uniforms you have to buy for work. These are considered business expenses and can be listed as a write-off on your taxes, which will save you money come tax season.

How to Dress Like a Billionaire

Like Steve Jobs did before him, Facebook CEO Mark Zuckerburg wears almost the exact same thing every day: a grey t-shirt, jeans, and sneakers or sandals. He's said in interviews that wearing the same outfit every day helps him avoid **decision fatigue**, so he has more time and energy leftover to focus on more important tasks.

Top Ten Dos & Don'ts of Business Attire

The following tips are helpful guidelines to keep in mind when selecting what to put on in the morning before heading to work—although remember that your company may have different dress code policies. When in doubt, check with your HR representative or boss.

1. **DON'T** wear revealing clothing. This typically means no shorts, no skirts or dresses shorter than knee length, and no low-cut or strapless shirts. Hint: when you lift your arms over your head or bend over, you should not reveal your lower back or stomach.
2. **DO** keep it simple. A flattering, modest, and understated outfit worn with confidence usually goes a long way. Avoid flashy scarves, colors and prints, hairdos, or jewelry.
3. If your company requires you to wear a uniform or protective equipment (such as helmets, masks, goggles, gloves, or gowns), **DO** be sure to wear them. Likewise, if your company requests that you wear a name tag, always place it on your upper torso so that it can be easily read by others.
4. **DON'T** wear clothes that are stained, torn, wrinkled, or unclean.
5. **DON'T** wear clothing that displays text, images, and/or competing brand names.
6. **DON'T** wear too much perfume or cologne. If you work in healthcare, wearing any kind of scent other than deodorant may even be strictly prohibited: this is to protect patients who are sensitive to fragrances and chemicals.

7. **DO** keep your nails short, clean, and neatly trimmed. If you wear polish, avoid bright and flashy colors. Do not wear fake nails.
8. **DO** wear comfortable and clean shoes. Keep in mind that you may work in a facility that requires closed-toe shoes only.
9. **DO** participate in dress-up or dress-down days. Many companies have dress-down days or encourage their employees to wear special clothes or costumes on certain holidays. Participating in these days can be a fun way to show company support and build rapport with your colleagues. Just be sure that the clothes you wear are still presentable. That is, you probably shouldn't wear sweatpants or wrinkly shirts on dress-down days. Likewise, you shouldn't wear revealing or offensive clothing, masks, or face paint on dress-up days.
10. **DO** bring a sweater or cardigan to work so that you have something warm to wear if you get cold. Depending on the type of work you do, you may want to leave an extra pair of clean clothes at work in case the outfit you have on becomes dirty or soiled.

Your Clothes Can Influence Others— and Even You

Dressing professionally not only makes you *look* professional, it can make you *feel* professional, too. Psychological research has found that dressing well can influence your mental and physical states. For example, wearing a nice suit can make you feel more confident, and may even improve your abstract thinking, which is important for things like creativity and problem-solving.

Being smart and consistent about the way you dress can also help you develop your own personal brand. For instance, the late founder of Apple, Steve

When in a practical or dusty environment, workers should wear clothing appropriate to the job in hand. This employee is suitably dressed for a day's work at a do-it-yourself store.

The dress code for some companies, particularly creative ones, is often more relaxed than in, for example, banking. However, this is not an excuse to be scruffy or unkempt. If casual attire is allowed, it should still be clean, well-pressed, and fitting to the environment.

Jobs, was famous for always wearing his hallmark outfit: a black mock turtleneck, blue jeans, dark socks, and New Balance sneakers. This helped solidify his iconic image within the technology and business world. Plus, it made getting ready for work in the morning much simpler!

Other famous people known for wearing the same outfit most of the time include Albert Einstein, singer Johnny Cash, Dean Kamen (the inventor of the Segway), and fashion designer Vera Wang.

So if you have a favorite item of clothing that is appropriate for work, feel free to buy it in multiple sets or multiple colors. Having less choice of what to wear can actually save you time in the morning. Plus, wearing the same thing every day can help you develop a signature style that can make you more memorable to clients, customers, and colleagues.

Personal Presentation: Dressing, Cleanliness & Good Manners

A Note on Keeping a Tidy Workspace

Creating and maintaining a professional image at work requires more than just clean clothing, of course. You should also strive to keep your workspace tidy and clean, too. Whether you have a locker, desk, or whole office, aim to always keep things organized and neat. In the next chapter, you'll learn about this in greater detail, including how to develop good organizational skills and why being tidy and clutter-free is so beneficial for you in the workplace.

Keep your workstation clean and tidy—your coworkers won't want to see your desk piled high with files and discarded items. When you have finished a job, file it away before starting another.

Good Manners Cost Nothing—but Bad Manners Could Cost You a Lot!

No matter how nicely you are dressed or how tidily you maintain your workspace, you will not earn anyone's respect on the job if you fail to have good manners.

At best, having bad manners can make people not want to work with you or be around you. At worst, bad manners can cause you and your company to lose paying customers, or cost you your job.

At its very core, having good manners on the job is what good etiquette is all about. This includes things like showing up on time, being positive, honest, and helpful—and of course wearing clean and respectable clothing.

Text-Dependent Questions

1. Where can you find out about your company's dress code policy?

2. Why does Mark Zuckerburg always wear the same clothing?

3. Name five ways to show that you are professional and have good manners while on the job.

Research Project

Create an ideal outfit for wearing to a job interview or on your first day at a new job. You can search for and save photos of clothing you find online, or else cut out photos from a magazine. The outfit you choose should be comfortable, decent, professional, flattering, and appropriate for your job of choice. Get creative and have a little fun! It can be exciting to imagine yourself as the professional you want to be someday.

Words to Understand

efficient: performing in the best possible manner with the least waste of time and effort; "doing things the right way"

productive: achieving a significant amount or result; producing a large quantity of goods or commodities

time management: the ability to use one's time productively, especially at work

Don't be late for work! This is disrespectful to your employer and other members of staff. If you arrive late due to an unfortunate circumstance, remember to apologize to your boss and explain the reason for your lateness.

Chapter Three
Timekeeping, Organization & Productivity

Aside from maintaining good manners and proper physical appearance, being **productive** at work is a huge part of proper workplace etiquette. Why? Producing quality and relevant work in a reasonable amount of time is very important to your bosses, colleagues, customers, and, most especially, to you.

Being Productive Can Increase Customer Satisfaction

Consider your customer first. Your customer is someone who is expecting to receive a specific product or service from you. By being productive, you're helping her get what she wants more quickly. This is an essential component of good customer service.

With good service, a customer is more likely to be loyal to you and your company. This probably means he'll be more likely to do business with you again, or recommend you to his friends and family. Word-of-mouth referrals are an important part of company promotion (marketing) in our modern age. In addition to talking with loved ones in person or on the phone, people can also share their experiences on social media platforms. This can help improve your reputation with hundreds or even thousands of new people who may become customers of yours in the future—all (or largely) because you provided a great service or product to your current clients in a speedy and friendly way.

Useful Tips for Good Customer Service
* Be a good listener
* Identify and anticipate a customer's needs
* Make a customer feel important and appreciated
* Know how to apologize
* Give more than is expected

Customers Rule!

According data collected by the cloud service company New Voice Media, US companies are losing about $62 billion a year due to poor customer service. That's a lot of income lost due to unhappy customers! Much of that money could be saved if employees and companies strove to increase their productivity and thus improve customer satisfaction.

How to Improve Your Productivity at Work

Productive Workplaces Are Happy Workplaces

Research shows that the most successful companies tend to have employees who are interested in their work and more productive on the job. This can seem a bit like a chicken-or-the-egg scenario. Which came first: happy employees or productive employees? In other words, does enjoying your work make you more productive? Or does being more productive make your work more enjoyable?

As it turns out, it could be a bit of both. Employees who work efficiently and effectively tend to find their work more rewarding. Being more satisfied by their jobs can make employees more effective, focused, and dedicated. This creates a virtuous circle.

As an employee, doing the right things and doing the right things well should be among your top priorities at work. If you're not sure what the "right things" are, ask your boss. It's better to have a clear idea of what's expected of you than waste company time on things that don't matter.

Being productive shows your colleagues that you are a team player who is committed to helping the company run more efficiently. Coworkers who see you as productive may be more likely to offer you help in return. You earn their respect, plus you prove that you are a valuable employee since you can get more work done in a shorter amount of time. This can literally save your company money, as well as improve the relationships you have with your colleagues.

Helpful Tips for Time Management, Organizing & Staying Focused

So how can you be productive? There are many ways you can improve your productivity, become more effective and **efficient**, and increase your ability to focus while at work. Here are a few helpful tips on **time management** and staying organized, some of which are from author Helene Segura of *The Inefficiency Assassin*.

Maintain an Organized Workspace

It's hard to be productive when you have to waste time looking for important documents or something to write with. So clean off your desk. Use folders, drawers, and binders to organize paper. Place the items you use the most within easy reach at all times.

Everything in your work area should have a designated place. When you're finished using something, be sure to return it to the spot you took it from. If you use a computer or laptop, make sure your desktop is clear of any clutter.

Create electronic folders to store and organize important files. Once every three to six months, go through your folders and properly dispose of unneeded papers and documents.

Prioritize Your Important Tasks

Every day, you should have a clear idea of what your most important tasks are at work. Write these tasks down in order of importance. Avoid writing down too many tasks or "to-dos," since this can overwhelm you. If you have several important tasks, do the most important ones first. Tackle each task one at a time as trying to multitask can cause errors and decrease your efficiency. If you're not sure which task is most important, ask yourself: "What one thing could I do (or not do) that would make every other task easier or no longer necessary?"

You can also prioritize your paperwork and mail in the same way. Don't just stick all of your papers in one pile or drawer. Organize them in order of priority. Any paperwork that requires action from you (such as making a phone call or performing certain a task) should be kept close by. Paperwork that contains useful or

Keep information held on your computer as tidy as possible. Each project or job should have its own filing system. In large companies, computers are backed up regularly on a daily basis to avoid loss of data. However, smaller companies rely on individuals to do their own backups. If in doubt, seek technical advice.

Deal with your email on a regular basis. In the workplace, you may received hundreds of emails a week, so it's vital to keep on top of them. Email is an important way of communicating with coworkers and customers. Don't allow emails to build up in your inbox as you may miss something important.

necessary information should be stored. Paperwork that you do not need should be recycled or shredded immediately.

If you're not sure about which tasks or what paperwork is important, ask your boss.

Be Smart When Checking Your Email

Email is an important way to communicate with coworkers and customers. But getting lost in your inbox can be a huge waste of your time. Try to only check your email at certain times of the day, like 9:00 a.m., 12:00 p.m., and 4:00 p.m. Also, set yourself a certain amount of time to get through your emails, such as ten or twenty minutes.

When you open your inbox, look for and immediately delete (don't open) emails that are spam, invites for events you can't or don't want to attend, emails about non-work-related matters or information that doesn't affect you or your department, and any other emails that you don't want or need. Archive emails that you may need to refer to in the future. Read and respond to emails that relate to your most important tasks first before responding to less important emails.

For a simple time-saving hack, remember: send less email, receive less email. Don't take the time to write, send, and/or read an email that could have been a two-minute conversation on the phone or in person.

The Dangers of Multitasking

Research shows that trying to do many things at once isn't actually a good time-management strategy. Multitasking can make you *less* efficient and *more* stressed out, and can even lower productivity by as much as 40 percent! So instead, tackle one task at a time and give it your full attention.

Use a Diary and/or Checklists for Regular Projects and Tasks

A checklist is a useful tool at work. It ensures that you complete all the necessary steps for your most important tasks. It can also prevent you from procrastinating. A good checklist includes everything that you'll need to complete a task, from start to finish. Keep your

checklist handy while you're working on a task, so you can easily refer to it as you go. That way, you won't waste time worrying about whether you forgot something.

You can use pen and paper or digital applications to keep your notes. Some popular digital methods for note-taking include Evernote, Microsoft Word, Notepad (on most devices), and task apps including Toodledo. Be sure to date your notes and diary entries.

Keeping a diary, whether it be traditional or digital, will help you in planning your schedule. In a busy workplace, relying on memory alone will invariably lead to missed appointments or double-bookings.

Timekeeping, Organization & Productivity

Avoid Time Wasters

Many things at work can be a drain on your ability to focus and produce quality work. This includes things like waiting for other people, long meetings, dealing with technical difficulties, wasting time on irrelevant or low-priority work, and using the Internet for social media and other non-work-related interests. Avoid these things as much as possible.

On the flip side, not wasting time doesn't mean you should lock yourself in your office and never leave for eight hours at a time. Taking a break may not *seem* like it would help productivity, but it's actually important for your ability to focus and retain information. Be sure to stand up at least once per hour for a brief stretch. If you complete a task, take a quick break and celebrate. Equally, if you feel yourself wanting to procrastinate, allow yourself a quick walk to the water fountain so that you can return to your desk feeling refreshed.

Leave office chat until break time. Constantly talking to workmates about matters not related to your work reduces your productivity and will annoy your boss and other members of staff, who many be trying to concentrate on their work.

Self-Care Is Key for Productivity

To be a productive employee at work, you also have to be a healthy person *outside* of work. Be sure that you maintain a healthy work/life balance. That is, avoid spending 80+ hours per week at the office. More time on the job doesn't always mean more work gets done.

Taking care of your health can make you a better and more productive employee for several reasons: you won't have to take as many sick days, you'll be able to focus better at work and you'll have more energy while at work.

So take care of your mental, physical, and emotional health. Do things outside of work that you enjoy. Be sure to exercise, get enough sleep, drink plenty of water, and spend time with loved ones. Avoid consuming too many stimulants, like coffee or sugary energy drinks, as these can make you crash at work and become mentally foggy and unfocused.

Lastly, if you've earned vacation time—take it! Research shows that people tend to be more energized, refreshed, and productive after they return from vacation. Sometimes, taking time for yourself is just what you need to make better use of time while you're on the job.

Text-Dependent Questions

1. Why is good customer service essential to a business?

2. When organizing your office space, where should you keep the supplies that you use most often?

3. Name three reasons why taking care of your health can make you a better employee.

Research Project

Do an online search for ways to improve productivity at work. Write a two-page report on some of these techniques or skills (you can include ones listed in this chapter as well). Explain why you think being more productive will make you a more valuable employee at your future job.

Words to Understand

mentor: an experienced and trusted advisor

micromanage: to try to control all the parts of some activity, no matter how small these parts are

workplace environment: the overall "vibe" or feeling of a workplace that has a big impact on an employee's level of productivity, quality of work, and overall job satisfaction

As you progress in your career, you may have to interact with other colleagues and clients during meetings. Always make notes of what's been discussed, so that you can keep accurate records to refer to later.

Chapter Four
Respect for Colleagues, Clients & Suppliers

Productivity is so important on the job that it may be tempting to just keep your head down, mind your own business, and get your work done. This may be appropriate in some situations. But you should also expect and welcome the reality that at almost any job you'll have to frequently engage with other people. This includes other coworkers, supervisors, clients, and suppliers.

Because workplaces often require teamwork and lots of interpersonal interaction, it's wise to develop healthy relationships with your coworkers and clients. Fortunately, presenting yourself in a respectful way does not have to take a lot of time. It's really all about practicing good etiquette. Aside from improving the relationships with the people you encounter on a daily basis, striving for great etiquette will make you a more valuable employee.

Respecting Colleagues & Clients

Projecting yourself as a respectful person can create a healthier **workplace environment**, where everyone can feel safe, valued, and inspired. Treating people respectfully, especially your customers, can also make a positive impact on your company's financial success and reputation, too.

Here are some of the most basic rules of workplace etiquette. Keep in mind that you should strive to show this level of respect to anyone you meet, both in the workplace and outside of it.

Be polite and friendly to customers, this will make them feel important to your business, which they are, of course.

Respect for Colleagues, Clients & Suppliers

Be Honest

When in doubt, tell the truth. Don't lie to colleagues or clients about errors you've made. It's perfectly normal to have a few blunders during your career. If you don't own up to your mistakes as soon as possible, then a small problem could become a big one.

Another part of being honest is asking for help when you need it. If you recognize someone in the office as a person with more experience and knowledge than you, consider asking them to be your **mentor**. A mentor is someone who you can turn to for help with challenging projects and tasks. He or she is there to help you problem-solve, develop new skills, and guide your overall on-the-job development. Just remember that mentors have busy work schedules, too. So always be respectful of their time.

Be Considerate

Your coworkers are busy, just like you. Do not waste their time by being late or arriving unprepared for a meeting. Equally, do not waste their time by interrupting them when they are with another colleague or client, by sending them too many emails, or talking to them about non-work-related matters when they are trying to focus.

Your customers' time is equally important. Respond to their emails or return their phone calls as promptly as you can. Even a quick message such as, "I got your email and am working on the problem. I'll get back to you as soon as I can," can be a great way to let your customer know they've been heard and are being looked after.

Finding a Mentor

If you are in a leadership role, do not try to **micromanage** colleagues who are working under you. Show them that you trust them by allowing them to make decisions for themselves. Give them the tools and resources they need to get their work done, then give them the space to do it.

It should go without saying that you should not steal your coworker's lunch! Being considerate also means respecting other people's personal belongings.

Lastly, if you're sick, stay home. Don't put your colleagues' health at risk by coming to work when you have the cold, flu, or some

Do You Trust the People You Work With?

Data collected by research scientists suggests that 38 percent of millennials (people born between 1980 and 1994) trust their boss "a lot," while 8 percent say they do not trust their boss "at all." As the next generation enters the workforce, it'll be important to find ways to help employees and employers build trust in each other.

Show consideration for others by not coming to work if you have an infectious disease, such as a cold or cough. Your coworkers will not thank you for it! If you feel well enough to work, however, suggest to your boss that you'd like to work from your home for a few days. Your boss will appreciate your commitment.

Whatever your occupation, being as helpful and courteous to customers as you can is vital to a successful business. A customer will remember good treatment and will invariably return.

other contagious condition. Besides, nobody enjoys sitting next to a person who is coughing, sneezing, and blowing their nose all day.

Be Fair

Do not participate in office gossip. If you hear someone around you gossiping or saying rude things about someone, simply do not participate in the conversation. If necessary, remove yourself from the area.

Handle negative customer reviews and customer complaints with respect, patience, and decency. Avoid blaming the customer for their own dissatisfaction with something. If you need help handling a difficult client, talk to your boss or mentor.

Be Helpful and Generous

The more you help other people, the more likely it is that other people will help you. Offer your insights and expertise if you see someone struggling with a problem or task.

When it comes to customer satisfaction, being helpful and generous is crucial to good business. In fact, data collected by the research company Forrester found that as many as 72 percent of companies surveyed said that improving customer satisfaction was their number one priority. Do your part by taking every chance you get to help your customers. Going the extra mile can really make a big difference in how happy your customer is with the product or service you provide.

Be Polite

Are you treating others the way you want to be treated? Do you talk to your coworkers with the same level of respect that you would talk to an elder? You do not necessarily have to be formal all the time, but you should still practice your basic "please" and "thank-yous." Lead

Remember that the workplace is not an environment for gossip, which can hurt a coworker's feelings. If you feel bullied or uncomfortable about how a coworker is treating you, do not suffer in silence, speak to HR or your boss about it.

by example and be polite with everyone you meet, from custodial staff to the president of your company.

It's not necessary to personally like everyone you work with, but you can still be courteous. If you need to vent about a frustrating coworker, feel free to do so outside of work with a family member, friend, or therapist.

Do not bring drama into the workplace, and be sure to leave your emotions out of your interactions with clients. Work life and personal life are both important, but in most cases are best kept separate.

A well-run meeting is the perfect opportunity for sharing information and brainstorming. Ideally, the meeting should have a clear leader who will follow an agenda. This can prevent things from going off-topic.

Looking at your cell phone or showing a lack of interest during a meeting is very bad manners. This is very disrespectful to your other coworkers and could even get you fired from your job.

Mastering the Meeting

Depending on the type of job you get, you may need to attend meetings throughout your typical work week. Meetings can be useful if they are run well. The meeting is a perfect opportunity to share a lot of information with many people at once. Plus, meetings can be a place to brainstorm ideas that may be used to help solve a problem that the company is currently facing.

But far too often meetings are drawn out, redundant, unproductive, and big time wasters. If you don't behave professionally in a meeting (large or small), it doesn't show respect to your colleagues.

Ideally, every meeting at work will have a clear leader or someone who is in charge. This can prevent things from going off-topic or people from arguing over decisions. Some companies may also allocate specific roles among the group present, including timekeeper

Respect for Colleagues, Clients & Suppliers

(someone who watches the clock to ensure the meeting doesn't go on too long) and scribe (someone who writes down notes to share later with the attendees and anyone else who needs the information).

Even if you aren't the leader of a meeting, there are still things you can do to show respect for your colleagues who are there with you.

- Be on time.
- Leave your phone on silent, not on vibrate.
- Prepare ahead so you are ready to participate fully.
- Be present at the meeting. Pay attention and do not multitask.
- Avoid interrupting people. Instead, listen actively to the conversation and speak up when appropriate.
- If you are confused about something, ask. Chances are, other people may have the same question. This can be a great way to bring clarity to your team.
- Be sure that you are clear on the accepted rules regarding food and drink at work meetings. It may be acceptable in some instances and not in others.
- If you don't need to be there for the entire meeting, ask your boss or supervisor ahead of time if you can excuse yourself early. This way, you can get back to more important work duties without appearing rude.

Suppliers Are the Company's Lifeblood, So Handle With Care

A supplier—or a company that provides your place of employment with inventory and supplies—should be treated with just as much respect as your customers. After all, companies that provide you with goods and services are necessary to ensure that the office runs efficiently and effectively. Miscommunication between companies and their suppliers can lead to challenges like late or missing work orders, an inadequate supply of office equipment, or even a bad reputation on the part of the organization you work for.

If your job requires you to interact with suppliers, such as paper goods companies, food delivery companies, medical supply companies, and construction companies, be sure to use your good etiquette practices. Remember, these organizations want your business as much as you want theirs. Specifically, suppliers appreciate it when you:

- Give realistic time frames for delivery of a product or completion of a service
- Acknowledge that you've received a quote (estimated cost of a particular job or service) after you've asked for one, and then let them know if and why you choose to go with a different supply company

- Work with them to resolve an issue instead of immediately and suddenly canceling orders and dropping them as a supplier
- Pay the dues owed on time

Having good workplace etiquette is about being respectful of other people's time, values, feelings, energy, and personal space and belongings. So whether you're new to a job or are planning on getting one in the near future, do your best to be helpful, kind, and to make people smile. It can make a big difference in your overall satisfaction and success, let alone improving your workplace environment.

Text-Dependent Questions

1. Give three specific examples of how to show respect to a customer, coworker, or supplier.

2. About what percentage of businesses say that improving customer satisfaction is their top priority?

3. What are three ways to show proper etiquette during a work meeting?

Research Project

What are the traits of an ideal employee? Do you see any of these traits in yourself? Choose between five and six traits to focus on and write a few sentences describing a time in your life when you exhibited each of those traits.

Words to Understand

diplomatic: having or showing an ability to deal with people in a sensitive and effective way

social capital: quality relationships among people who work in a particular organization, which allows that organization to function effectively

tactful: the quality of having sensitivity in dealing with others or with a difficult situation

If you have any concerns about anything to do with the running of the business, speak to your boss. If it's a personal matter talk to the HR department.

Chapter Five
How to Be Tactful
& Diplomatic

When you're an adult, you'll spend a lot of your time at work. No matter how well you present yourself, how wisely you manage your time, or how respectfully you treat your colleagues, clients, and suppliers, you are bound to deal with challenging situations from time to time. Part of having good etiquette is knowing how to handle yourself in an effective and considerate way, even in the face of adversity.

Perhaps another colleague is doing something unethical or illegal. Perhaps a client is unhappy and upset with your service. Perhaps you want to ask for a raise, or want to leave your current job altogether. These and other situations are not uncommon. But just because certain situations can make people a little uncomfortable it doesn't mean they shouldn't be addressed and resolved.

Why? Because in the business world (like in other areas of life) a problem doesn't usually just go away if it's ignored.

Some of the best ways to effectively solve friction in the workplace are to be **tactful** and **diplomatic**. In other words, you need to be sensitive to other people's emotions and needs. You need to be able to tell the truth while also being mindful of how other people feel. Doing so makes you appear mature and credible. It establishes you as a member of the workplace who has good character and good integrity. Your good qualities and manners can improve your satisfaction and overall happiness on the job. They will also increase the chance that you'll get noticed for promotions and other opportunities for career advancement.

Tact and Diplomacy 101: Basic Rules for Handling Sticky Situations

Being tactful and diplomatic are important communication skills that help you understand other people

Running a meeting or presentation can be a daunting task. The trick is to prepare what you have to say beforehand. Once something has been said, you can't take it back. Remember to be a good listener too.

and be understood better yourself. It is also an important way to build **social capital** so that your company will function more effectively overall. The following are some general guidelines for maintaining a necessary level of tact and diplomacy on the job. These can be applied to a difficult situation at work or even elsewhere in your life:

Think Before You Speak

Choose your words carefully. Once something has been said, you can't take it back. So do everything you can to share your thoughts in a respectful way.

State facts before feelings. Do your best not to react to situations emotionally. You are more likely to act rudely or say things you'll later regret if you let your emotions take over the conversation.

Try to mentally rehearse a challenging conversation beforehand. This can help you avoid emotional reactivity and improve your ability to express your concerns, thoughts, and suggestions.

Taking the time to think before you speak can also give the other person time to respond and share their views. By being a good listener, you are being a good communicator, too.

Taking care of your health is an important part of communicating better. If you are stressed, overtired, run-down, or unwell, you are far more likely to be emotionally reactive instead of in control and gracious.

On-The-Clock Time

The average person will spend about 90,000 hours of their life at work! For a typical seventy-five-year-old person, this equals approximately 13 percent of their lifetime, or about 20 percent of their waking hours.

Be as Direct as Possible

It is possible to stand up for yourself without being rude or dismissive of other people. If something is bothering you, speak up. Figure out the right time and the right place for bringing up an issue or complaint.

Ensure that your body language is open, and not threatening or dismissive. Do not cross your arms, do not point, do not cross your legs, and do not fiddle with your hands. These nonverbal cues will not make you appear direct or diplomatic, but rather insecure or aggressive.

Instead, make eye contact. Maintain good posture. Smile when possible and where appropriate.

Make sure that you are bringing up your concerns with the right person, too. Ideally, this person should be someone directly involved in the issue, or someone who has the power to resolve the issue. You should not talk about sensitive issues or problems with people who are not involved. This can be misconstrued as gossip, which is toxic for the workplace.

Remember to start sentences with "I" instead of "You." People often get defensive if they feel they are being criticized, and "You" statements often sound harsh, even if you aren't intending them to be.

Look for Solutions, Not Ways to Be "Right"

Work with the other person to try to find a "win-win" solution to your problem. This may not always be possible, but there is usually a way to help everyone get what they want or at least accept the end result.

Ask questions like, "What can I do to help?" or "How can we figure this out together?" This shows respect for the other person and creates a sense of teamwork.

Realize that you are only seeing things from your side of the story. Listen and create space for other people involved in the situation to state their part. They may have insights or knowledge that you weren't aware of that can help clarify the situation.

How to be Tactful & Diplomatic

A Quotation to Think About

"Respond intelligently, even to unintelligent treatment."

—Lao Tzu

Common Work Challenges That Require Tact & Diplomacy

Being tactful and diplomatic is about helping yourself and others feel successful, valued, and understood. Certain situations may require unique strategies and skills to ensure that this is achieved.

Receiving Feedback

Getting feedback from your supervisors or bosses can be an uncomfortable experience. But trust that their suggestions can make you a more effective and valued employee. Try to listen with an open mind, and remember that nobody is perfect. Everyone has areas where they can improve.

During a performance review or feedback session, ensure that the tone of your voice and your body language remains open and relaxed. Make eye contact and don't cross your arms.

Be sure to ask questions like, "How can I do better at this?" or "What can I do to improve this?" Being engaged with the conversation and interested in improving your skills shows that you are mature and that you value your role in the company.

Lastly, be sure to thank your employer for offering feedback. This is respectful and can also show that you are a person your employer can trust to handle tricky situations with class.

Helping a Dissatisfied Customer

When a customer is reacting emotionally to a problem they have with you, your company, or your service or product (whether real or imagined), it can be extremely difficult not to take it personally. Try to consider that this person is simply frustrated and taking it out on you. It is not necessarily a reflection on you as a person, but simply a reality of dealing with interpersonal communication.

Remain calm. Take a few deep breaths before entering a conversation with an angry client.

Do not interrupt the client and instead allow them to speak freely. Show that you are listening by maintaining good eye contact and body language. When they are done talking, briefly summarize what they just said to show you were listening.

Be sympathetic. Say something to show that you understand where they are coming from. Whether the customer's complaint is legitimate is not as important as whether you show the client that they have been heard and understood. "I hear what you're saying" and

If a customer has a complaint about your company, first apologize on behalf of the company, then find out what the problem is. If you cannot sort it out yourself, ask someone in a senior position to assist you.

How to be Tactful & Diplomatic

"I can see how that would be frustrating" can be helpful phrases to calm an angry customer.

If you're wrong about something or made a mistake, acknowledge it. You don't need to grovel and beg for forgiveness; simply recognize your mistake and come up with a solution to remedy it. Be sure to follow up with the client at a later time to express your gratitude for their continued business. Try a note like this: "Thank you for your business and your feedback. Customers like you are what make our company better. Please let me know if I can help in any other way."

Be classy, considerate, and graceful.

Asking Someone to Stop Chatting or Gossiping

Sometimes, a coworker may be talking a lot while you are trying to work. Avoid the temptation to simply nod and occasionally smile while still trying to complete your task. Being distracted could hurt the quality of your work. Plus, by not actively listening, you are not being respectful to the other person.

Avoid talking negatively about a coworker. Getting drawn into this form of conversation is bad for all parties involved. It is important to make it clear that you do not wish to speak about a person behind their back.

Also, do not assume that the person will eventually take the hint and leave. You can be direct and honor your needs while also being polite. For example, try: "I'd love to hear more about this, but I really want to focus on my work right now. Can we chat another time?" This way, you're setting a clear boundary while also acknowledging the other person's desire to talk and bond with you.

If a person is gossiping or talking negatively about someone, try hinging the conversation on yourself. "I'm making an effort to cut back on talking negatively about other people, so I'd rather not talk about this." In other cases, you may need to take more direct approach. Try: "I don't want to talk poorly about someone behind their back" or "We should talk about this when she's here. We don't know the whole story."

Declining an Invitation

You shouldn't feel obligated to go to an event that you don't really want to attend just because a coworker invited you. That said, don't say you will or might be there simply because you think declining will hurt their feelings or seem rude.

Instead, sandwich your "no" with positivity. You can start by thanking the person for inviting you, then simply state that you won't be able to attend. Finish with a polite thought, such as, "I'm sure it will be a lovely event," "I hope everyone has a great time," "Can't wait to see the pictures," or "Let me know how it goes."

Text-Dependent Questions

1. On average, how many hours of your life will you spend at your job?

2. What are three ways you can prepare for having a difficult conversation?

3. Someone is gossiping about another coworker at work. What is a tactful way you can ask this person to stop or else remove yourself from the conversation?

Research Project

Research the phrase "active listening." Write a two-page report on what it means to be an active listener and why it is so important for communication.

Words to Understand

faux pas: an embarrassing or tactless act or remark in a social situation

job satisfaction: the extent to which a person's hopes, desires, and expectations about the employment they are engaged in are fulfilled

job security: the probability that a given individual will be able to keep their job and avoid becoming unemployed

Business lunches are a great way to bond with customers. While it is not necessary to be as formal as you would in the office, your behavior and use of language should reflect the importance of the lunch you are attending.

Chapter Six
Self-Control, Emotions & Social
——— Occasions in the Workplace ———

Proper work etiquette requires good behavior in and out of the office. To be as successful as possible in your career, you should strive to always do what your best judgment tells you is the right thing in any given moment.

Companies often offer opportunities for their employees to bond and socialize outside of the workplace. These may be sanctioned "team-building" activities, such as seminars or workshops. Sometimes, companies will extend invitations to family members of employees in order to celebrate certain holidays, build rapport, raise morale, or honor certain milestones within the company.

In other cases, you may choose to engage with your coworkers on a more informal basis. Perhaps you and your group will want to get together for a meal after work one day. Or you may decide to join a club or sports team together.

No matter what brings you together outside the office, these extracurricular activities can be a great way to bond with your colleagues and release some work-related stress. However, don't let the relaxed atmosphere fool you. Work-related social occasions still require you to present yourself in a positive, trustworthy, and respectful light.

In other words, you can still have fun at an office holiday party, but it should certainly be more reserved compared to a private holiday meal with your closest friends and family.

Tips for Safe Socializing With Colleagues & Bosses

Whether you are relaxing during your lunch hour, grabbing a meal together after work, or participating in a company-sanctioned

There are times throughout the year when it's traditional to socialize with work colleagues. It could be to celebrate a holiday or the winning of an account. Whatever the occasion, enjoy yourself, but don't drink too many alcoholic beverages, and remember to treat senior coworkers with respect.

event, it is important to keep in mind these helpful hints while socializing with your colleagues:

Be Comfortable With Saying No

Remember, it's better to politely decline an invitation than to respond with a "maybe," or worse, say you'll be there and then not show up at all. If there is a work-related social occasion that isn't mandatory, and which you do not wish to attend, simply tell the person who invited you that while you appreciate being asked along, you won't be able to make it. Don't feel the need to make up an excuse or reason, and certainly don't lie about why you're not going to be there. Remember to finish with a kind expression like this: "I'm sure the party is going to be great. Hope you have a wonderful time."

Watch Your Language

It's normal to let down your guard when you're in a relaxed social setting. However, if you curse in your private life, make sure to keep it in your private life.

Sure, there may be some exceptions to the rule. But don't take a gamble. Foul language, crass jokes, and lewd topics have no place in the workplace, whether you're actually in the office or not.

Dress With Class

Depending on the event, you may not be expected to wear formal office attire. That said, you still should wear clothes that are relatively modest and flattering. The same goes for jewelry, perfume or cologne, and other accessories. Feel free to show off a bit more of your personal style, but reserve your wildest tastes for other times.

Enjoy Food and Drink in Moderation

Once you've reached the legal drinking age, you'll be free to consume alcohol if you wish to do so. However, use caution when drinking adult beverages at work-related events. Getting drunk is a major **faux pas** that can be embarrassing at best, or damaging to your **job security,** reputation, and career at worst.

Avoid Work-Related Gossip

Yes, you can still have fun! You shouldn't be afraid to be social with your coworkers or even bosses. As already mentioned, this is a great way to build social capital and boost morale within the company, both of which can increase your productivity and overall **job satisfaction**.

Social occasions are for socializing. So use these occasions to get to know your colleagues better. Ask about their families, their hobbies, or any other common interests you may have. Avoid work-related talk and gossip, however.

Interoffice Romance: A Slippery Slope

Most companies have specific guidelines regarding romantic relationships between employees. It is strictly prohibited in some businesses and permissible on a case-by-case

Mixing Business With Pleasure

It's old news to some, but people really do need reminders about how to behave appropriately when they mix business with pleasure. This is particularly the case if you're a new employee trying to put your best face forward at an office holiday party or other workplace event.

basis in others. Be sure to talk to your HR representative about your employer's policies on romantic relationships within the workplace, especially if you believe you have feelings for a colleague.

Remember that flirting with someone in the workplace can distract you and others. It can hurt your reputation and may make you appear less reliable and focused. Casual flirting, even if you think the other person is inviting it, may be deemed unwelcome. This can be considered sexual harassment, which is a serious problem.

In general, you should keep relationships with your colleagues strictly professional. If you're looking for romance, search for a connection outside the office so you're not running the risk of jeopardizing your career.

Office Extroverts vs. Office Introverts

According to psychological research, extroverts (people who are energized by social interaction) represent anywhere from 50 to 74 percent of the population. Introverts (people who are energized by alone time) represent anywhere from 16 to 50 percent.

Tips for Dining With Current or Prospective Clients

Sometimes, companies will ask you to entertain potential clients and business associates. The business lunch or dinner, whether formal or informal, is a common way to do this. If you've been chosen to take a client out to a meal, be sure to dress and behave professionally, and use proper dining etiquette to show that you have class.

Etiquette When Attending a Business Lunch

The following are a few basic dining etiquette tips that are perfect for the business lunch:

- Leave your napkin neatly folded in your lap.
- Unless you and the client are using technology to share information with each other directly at the table, keep your phone tucked away. Make sure it is turned on silent, and not on vibrate.
- Never talk while you have food in your mouth.
- Remember to be considerate of different cultures. If you are overseas or hosting an international traveler, make an effort to find out about that country's customs for dining.
- Be courteous to your guest at the end of the meal. If you or your company has invited them, pay for the meal (your employer will typically reimburse you). Before you leave, briefly summarize the topics discussed during the meal, and be sure to confirm any follow-up appointments or future next steps that are needed.

Text-Dependent Questions

1. What is the dress code for an office party?

2. What are two tips for safe socializing with your colleagues or boss?

3. List two reasons why flirting with someone in the office is bad etiquette.

Research Project

Do an online search on team-building activities for the workplace. Write a one-page report describing your favorite exercise, and list between three and five ways that team-building exercises can benefit coworkers.

Words to Understand

information technology (IT): The application of computers to store, study, retrieve, transmit, and manipulate data or information.

job satisfaction: The feeling of pleasure and achievement that you experience in your job.

leverage: The power to influence a person or situation to achieve a particular outcome.

Most large offices have a storeroom or cupboard where all the stationery and supplies are kept.

Chapter Seven
Appropriate Use of Office Equipment

So far, you've learned several major ways to show good etiquette in the workplace. Everything from the way you dress, to the way you organize your time and office, to the overall way you treat other people will have a major impact on your experience in your chosen career.

Having good etiquette can increase your **job satisfaction**. Acting professionally and being a team player feels good and mature, and can help you develop a stronger sense of confidence and self-esteem.

This, in turn, can make you more productive and more valuable to the company you work for. Over time, all this can help you **leverage** yourself when it comes to asking for a raise, competing for a promotion, or even applying for a new job.

Who knew? Being nice and considerate to others is a great way to improve your own happiness and well-being!

When it comes to workplace etiquette, the last piece of the puzzle is understanding how to use (or how not to use) office supplies and equipment. You may only think of office supplies like paper, pens, printer ink, or even computers and laptops as just the usual stuff you need to get your job done. While this is true, keep in mind that this equipment is also necessary for *other* people to get work done. Properly sharing, cleaning, storing, and using supplies shows that you have respect for your employers, suppliers, and fellow coworkers who are depending on these tools and resources to remain productive and efficient.

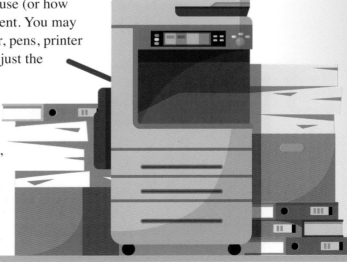

Appropriate Use of Office Equipment

Ten Tips for Office Equipment Use

1. Do not send or share sensitive or private information over unsecured Internet connections, including private email servers.

2. If you run out of something while you're using it, refill, replace, recharge, or replenish it. This includes simple things like refilling the stapler with staples, or the printer with paper. If you don't know how to refill something (like printer toner) or are not sure where to find a replacement, ask your office supply manager or other coworker who would know.

3. Avoid surfing the Internet for personal use. This includes things like checking private emails, looking at your social media accounts, and online shopping. Check with your supervisor or HR representative, since your company may even have a strict policy on Internet use.

4. Always dispose of sensitive documents in a secure way (e.g., delete or shred).

5. If you accidentally break or otherwise destroy something, fess up. If it was a genuine accident, your employer should understand. If you were clearly being careless, it is reasonable to expect some sort of financial or disciplinary consequences.

6. Properly sanitize any supplies according to policy directions. This is especially important during flu season or if you work in the healthcare field, where infection control and personal protective equipment is essential for the health of patients and staff.

A Simple Equipment Etiquette Guide

7. Ask yourself before you print: do you really need this information in hard copy? Avoid using too much paper, or too much of any supply for that matter. You usually need less than you think.

8. If Internet service is down or spotty, be respectful and patient with your company's **IT** team. Assume that they are doing the best they can to fix the problem. Getting frustrated will not make them work any faster.

9. Unless you have explicit permission, never bring office equipment (especially technology)

Social Media: The Great Time Drain

A survey from Salary.com reveals that 64 percent of employees report surfing the web at work using non-work-related websites, with the most common sites being Facebook, LinkedIn, and Amazon. Some organizations use time tracker software and site blocking to prevent this occurring.

Some companies will provide you with a company laptop, tablet, or smartphone. While some employers will allow them to be used for personal use, others may not. Make sure you know the rules.

Appropriate Use of Office Equipment

back to your home. This is disrespectful of other coworkers who may need the device and could potentially be misconstrued as an attempt to steal company property.

10. Don't be a slob! Just because your office may employ a custodial team doesn't mean you can leave a mess. Pick up after yourself. Wash your own dishes and clean out the microwave after you use it. It's respectful behavior, and shows that you take pride in your work and work space.

Respect Company Property, Respect Your Job, Respect Yourself & Others

The bottom line is that you should treat your company supplies the same way that you would want people to treat your personal belongings at home. Office supplies are not *your* supplies. They are company property and should be respected.

Using company property and company time to chat to your friends or surf the Internet shows a lack of respect for your employer. It also suggests to others that you are not doing your job properly.

The reality of the adult working world is that if you have a hard time showing self-control and integrity, you will probably not be able to hold a job for too long. Employers want to hire people they can trust to do their job without needing someone to keep tabs on them all the time. Employers also want employees who show a level of maturity, decency, and respectfulness toward everyone associated with the organization.

So, no matter what field you choose, always remember that your actions and words make a lasting impression on customers, colleagues, and bosses alike. It's up to you to ensure that the impression is a good one.

Text-Dependent Questions

1. What percentage of workers admit they waste time at work by using the Internet for non-work-related tasks?

2. You want to throw out a piece of paper that contains personal information (health, financial, or otherwise) about a client of your company. How should you dispose of this paper?

3. You are working on an assignment on a company laptop and want to finish it at home on your couch. You aren't sure if you have clearance to bring the computer home. What should you do?

Research Project

Study http://www.ifpo.org/resource-links/articles-and-reports/crime-violence-and-terrorism/employee-theft/ from the International Foundation for Protection Officers. Write a two-page essay about theft in the workplace, answering the following questions: What kinds of things do employees steal from their employers? Why do people steal from their employers? How can employee theft be prevented?

Series Glossary of Key Terms

appreciation	Gratitude and thankful recognition.
body language	Nonverbal communication through posture or facial expression.
bully	Overbearing person who habitually intimidates weaker or smaller people.
civil	Adhering to the norms of polite social intercourse.
clingy	Tending to stay very close to someone for emotional support.
common sense	Sound judgment based on simple perceptions of a situation.
compatible	Capable of existing together in harmony.
compliment	An expression of affection, respect, or admiration.
confidence	The state of being certain.
cyberbullying	The electronic posting of mean-spirited messages about a person.
empathy	Being aware of the feelings and thoughts of another.
eulogy	A commendatory oration or writing, especially in honor of one deceased.
faux pas	A social blunder.
frenemy	One who pretends to be a friend but is actually an enemy.
gossip	A person who habitually reveals personal facts about others.
grace	Disposition to act with kindness and courtesy.
inappropriate	Not suited for a purpose or situation.
initiative	The power to do something before others do.
inoculation	Injecting a vaccine to protect against or treat disease.
integrity	The quality of being honest and fair.
judgmental	Tending to judge people too quickly and critically.
lust	To have an intense desire or need.
manner	The way something is done or happens.
networking	The cultivation of productive relationships.
peer	One who is of equal standing with another.
poise	A natural, self-confident manner.
polite	Having or showing good manners or respect for others.
prioritize	To organize things so that the most important one is dealt with first.
procrastinate	To put off intentionally and habitually.
problem-solving	The process of finding a solution to a problem.
online	Connected to a computer.
relationship	The way in which two or more people are connected.
respect	To consider worthy of high regard.
RSVP	To respond to an invitation.
self-centered	Concerned solely with one's own needs.
socialize	Participate in social activities.
social media	Forms of electronic communications through which users share information, ideas, and personal messages.
staying power	Capacity of continuing without weakening.
sympathy	Caring about someone else's misfortune or grief.
tact	A keen sense of what to do or say without upsetting other people.

Further Reading

Christen, Carole. *What Color Is Your Parachute?* New York: Ten Speed Press, 2006.

Godin, Seth. *Linchpin: Are You Indispensable?* New York: Penguin Group, 2010.

Manecke, Kirt. *Smile & Succeed for Teens: A Crash Course in Face-to-Face Communication.* Milford, MI: Solid Press, 2014.

Pryce-Jones, Jessica. *Happiness at Work: Maximizing Your Psychological Capital for Success.* West Sussex, UK: Wiley-Blackwell, 2010.

Seglin, Jeffrey L., and Edward Coleman. *The AMA Handbook of Business Letters.* 4th edition. New York: American Management Association, 2012.

Segura, Helene. *The Inefficiency Assassin: Time Management Tactics for Working Smarter, Not Longer.* Novato, CA: New World Library, 2016.

Internet Resources

http://www.forbes.com *Forbes* is an American business magazine. Their website offers thousands of interesting articles on business, technology, entrepreneurship, leadership, and lifestyle.

https://knowitall.org Educational media content for kids K-12. Their section on career education offers videos, articles, and interactive games to help kids learn about careers, leadership, and more.

https://www.psychologicalscience.org The official website of the nonprofit organization committed to the advancement of scientific psychology and its use in daily life. Use this website to read about interesting studies on a wide variety of topics.

Publisher's note:
The websites listed on this page were active at the time of publication. The publisher is not responsible for websites that have changed their addresses or discontinued operation since the date of publication. The publisher will review and update the website list upon each reprint.

Index

Picture Credits

All images in this book are in the public domain or have been supplied under license by © Shutterstock.com.
To the best knowledge of the publisher, all images not specifically credited are in the public domain. If any image has been inadvertently uncredited, please notify the publisher, so that credit can be given in future printings.

Video Credits

Page 16 Rona Esteban: http://x-qr.net/1HHe, page 24 Andy Core: http://x-qr.net/1G5Z
page 32 Connect Professional Women's Network: http://x-qr.net/1GG8
page 44 Plainly Simple Studios: http://x-qr.net/1Dvm, page 52 Rothman Institute of Entrepreneurship: http://x-qr.net/1G3H, page 56 Etiquette Talk: http://x-qr.net/1HFm

About the Author

Sarah Smith is a freelance writer currently living and working in the Boston area. She is also a board-certified Doctor of Physical Therapy, licensed by the Commonwealth of Massachusetts. She attended Boston University, where she earned both her doctorate and, as an undergraduate, a bachelor of science in health studies.

Sarah has been writing for her entire life, and first became a published author at age fourteen, when she began contributing to a weekly column for her local newspaper. Since beginning her freelance writing career in earnest in 2014, Sarah has written over 1,500 articles and books. Her work covers a broad range of topics, including psychology and relationships, as well as physical and mental health.

Additionally, she has over fifteen years of professional experience working with typically developing and special-needs children, along with their families, in a variety of settings, including schools, pediatric hospitals, and youth-group fitness programs. She spent over thirteen years working as a private nanny and babysitter for families in both her hometown of Yarmouth, Maine, as well as in and around the great city of Boston. Sarah also has experience tutoring and leading teens and young adults as part of a variety of clinical internship programs for physical therapy.